Fifteen Ways to Calm Your Mind Without Driving Yourself Crazy

Coping with stress, anxiety, and PTSD

Dr. Joel F. Shults

Joelshults.com

DEDICATION

Time gets more precious with every passing moment. Thank you to my wife Cheryl for allowing me to invest some of our precious time in this work. Thank you to all the scholars and to all my friends who have taught me to remain calm by their example and counsel, especially the courageous men and women first responders I've been honored to know.

Joelshults.com

Introduction

Skip this if you want to. See? I'm already helping you decide to make choices to make your life easier!

I know why you're reading this book - it's either because you're trying to ready everything you can about dealing with stress, anxiety, negative thoughts, self-improvement, etc and this is just one more; or somebody thinks you're driving yourself crazy and thought this might help, or you're just starting to explore improving your life and this book popped up somewhere – or maybe you're trying to learn more about the subject in order to help someone else.

Regardless of what brought you here, I am so glad to be sharing with you! I have been intentional in making this a short reading experience with some specific things you can do right away to improve your life. Notice I didn't say dramatically change your life. While some insight might indeed put you on a new life course, the reality of change includes the **inevitability**

of gradualness. Baby steps. A little better than yesterday, even a little better by tomorrow, with stalls and setbacks along the way.

Reading a lot of books on self-improvement or how to deal with stress and anxiety can drive you crazy. You can end up saying that the author doesn't really know what you're going through. They asks too much. It seems too simple or too hard or too complicated. In this short read, I'll just give you some quick strategies you might want to try without wearing out your psyche. You might find one or two or none or all of these fifteen strategies to be helpful. Just remember that it's not likely that you'll have a huge life difference immediately from some insight I provide. **I'm just hoping for some incremental step toward a quieter, more peaceful mind.**

One life management skill is adjusting your expectations from overly optimistic or pessimistic to attainable and realistic. When medicines are tested, researchers often find that the "fake" pill given shows a patient's improvement over no pill at all, or only slightly less effective than the real medicine! That's the placebo effect – the patient wants it to work, has been told it will work, so the body works at some mysterious level to make it work.

There can also be a "nocebo" effect, where a doctor urges the patient to understand the limitations of a medicine or procedure and, in an attempt to keep the patient from being disappointed if the outcome isn't positive, creates a low expectation and potentially self-fulfilling prophecy of failure.

I want to strike just the right balance for the reader. I can tell you that any one of these suggestions has made a big difference in people's lives. I can also assure you that, even though I've omitted lengthy citations of studies and research, each of these suggestions is backed by science. I can also tell you that these are my personal strategies that I've successfully used to push through challenging times in my own life. I can also tell you that it is your responsibility to measure and practice, with consistency and self-awareness and the support of others, any or all of these suggestions in order to take control of your well-being.

An important notice: This publication is not intended to diagnose or treat any illness or disorder. Persons with discomfort or distress should seek appropriate professional care and diagnosis.

PTSD, in particular, must be diagnosed by a licensed mental health professional using accepted diagnostic criteria. PTSD can be a complex condition complicated by co-occurring conditions that create challenges to treatment. Mere "stress management" is not treatment for PTSD, but stress management can be an important component, and is an important area of concern for care-givers and loved ones who support the PTSD sufferer.

Contact me at jshults@joelshults.com or at www.joelshults.com

Strategy # 1: Psychoeducation

During times of high stress and crisis, we can feel like we're literally going crazy. We might feel paralyzed, find it hard to breathe, and overwhelmed with sadness or anger or panic. As a first responder and chaplain, I've found that one of the most comforting things a person in crisis can hear is that they are acting within the realm of normal for the circumstance. In other words – you're not crazy.

That is a little example of **psychoeducation**, which is simply learning about your body and brain. This gives you some insight into human behavior enough to know whether you're acting within a normal range of human behavior.

"Normal" clearly varies from circumstance to

circumstance. Screaming and thrashing in the mall because your coupon is expired is not within the bounds of normal. Screaming and thrashing when the car you're driving has crashed and is on fire is normal.

Sometimes the discomfort we feel in our own skin is because we do recognize that our behavior is different from what is normal for the circumstances. Sometimes our behavior isn't normal, but seems normal to us, but since it is odd to others, we sense their disengagement or disapproval but we don't know why and that causes us to feel bad about ourselves. Sometimes the discomfort is because, while the behavior is in fact acceptably normal, those who have had power over us such as parents or partners, have caused us to be habitually self-critical and we end up defining ourselves as weird or dumb.

The human animal learns behavior by the process of imitation, part of what is often referred to as **mirroring**. This is imitating the behavior of those around us. We learn to smile from being smiled at in our adorable infancy. We develop a dependence on positive feedback and acceptance. This is normal and healthy.

We get rewarded for certain behavior and punished (or not rewarded) for other behavior. This behavior can be as subtle as a facial expression or the way we breathe or walk. A problem arises when behaviors, attitudes, habits, body movements, and just about anything that defines who we are gets over-examined, criticized, or rejected and this results in a brain response of anxiety. Anxiety is not always recognized and may manifest as a generally crappy feeling, unexplained anger, and depression.

Those are likely the feelings that are the reason you are reading this book.

The way I describe the brain's working is way too simple to be endorsed by scientists who have long words to describe these things, but it seems to be functionally accurate at a basic level. Everyone has heard of the **fight** or **flight** syndrome. It is my baseline for analyzing behavior, with the addition of the third "F" of **freeze**. I refer to this process as **F3**. Behavior is a result of thinking, and most of our thinking happens at a less than conscious awareness. Thinking, feeling, and acting are tied together in ways we don't usually clearly understand.

In fact, we don't need to understand or be aware of every input and process that the mind and body undergo because the part of our brain that makes us explicitly aware of what's going on simply would not be able to keep up with it all. Our brain, very conveniently, takes over so that we can act without the paralyzing effect of over-analysis.

Most of what we do is automatic, so habitual and routine that we literally take no thought of it. The things we do analyze can become better or worse for it. An athlete who analyzes her every move and motive can become incrementally better or can be crippled with self-awareness. We can end up like the centipede who was asked by a curious cricket how he knew which foot to move to make his graceful walk and ended up flailing on his back in confusion.

What if you used my simple F3 brain outline to consider your behavior? Let's explore the F3 a little further.

I label three areas of the brain that I call the **lizard brain**, the **linking brain**, and the **logic brain**. The logic brain is the part of our brain that we mistakenly think makes most of our daily decisions. It is based on facts, makes rational calculations based on pros and cons, and puts into motion behavior that acts in our best interests based on our moral foundation.

I say that we *think* that the logic brain is where we do our thinking. However, there is not enough space in that part of our brain to process the millions of pieces of data and sensory input at an awareness level. For example, we know that movies are stationary pictures shown in rapid sequence that we perceive as motion. Our brain "knows" what the pictures are meant to look like and sews them together in our mind to be lifelike motion. The brain also does this with our own eyes as we scan, filling in the blanks of our perception.

Consider what a complicated process walking or talking is. If you have any doubts just ask someone who has had to endure rehabilitation to relearn speech or movement. All those lessons as an infant have made walking and talking behaviors that require no conscious thought. For those with highly developed athletic skills, making a catch or throw or shot seems effortless because, if their activity is within the realm of normal activity for them, the calculations necessary to be successful come without conscious thought because they have already been made and rehearsed.

Where do these less-than-conscious-awareness thoughts and behaviors come from? That is the part that I call the linking brain. In it resides emotion and memory, which work together with the logic brain to make decisions both at the awareness and less than awareness level. It is the well to which both the logic and lizard brain go to inform behavior decisions.

Now let's talk about that lizard brain. The purpose of this part of your brain is to keep you alive for the next couple of minutes. **That is its only job**. Since it has this critical task, it has been given superpowers. **The lizard brain can take over all body systems in a crisis**, signaling a chemical dump for emergency powers to the rest of the body, and creating an instant response that bypasses or overrides the logic brain.

The result of this is magnificent in most life-threatening emergencies. It's the kind of thing that enabled my teenaged nephew to lift a car off my brother when the car he was working on fell off the jack and pinned him. It is what makes you run faster than you thought you could when chased. It is the cause of the feeling of shakiness and nausea after you pull off the roadway after a car crash or near miss.

Despite the lifesaving benefits of the lizard brain's work, there are two big problems. The first is that the lizard brain cares nothing about the fallout from its work. The second is that the lizard brain gets excited about a lot of things. Let me explore that a little bit.

The lizard brain gets your body ready for an F3 response by activating a cocktail of chemistry, that I'll just label generically as adrenaline, to flood your body. This chemistry changes everything. Any body function that doesn't contribute to your survival RIGHT NOW is reduced, shut down, or channeled to survival mode. Got food in your stomach? For a body taken over by the lizard brain, there is no need to digest food that may never be used. Thinking about sex? No need for that! Need to engage in some delicate movement with your fingers? Uh uh – we need that blood down in your leg muscles to run or kick. Got an infection brewing? Can't spare any white blood cells now!

You can see why stress is blamed for bad digestion, relationship or sex problems, fatigue, illness, high blood pressure, and on and on. Even when you're not in full-blown F3 you can be in a partial F3. One part of your brain is telling your body to get through the day and be a normal human being. The other part of your brain is saying WATCH OUT!

So, controlling your mind and body is essential to stress awareness and control. An amazing discovery of what makes this possible is that the brain can change. It has *plasticity*! You can learn new skills, get rid of bad habits, develop new capacities, and open new horizons, which means you can change the way you think, feel, and act!

Strategy # 2: Psychometrics

One baseline of mental and physical health is the quality of our interpersonal relationships. The psychoanalyst might declare that our real conflicts are with ourselves, but if we spend all our time in self-reflection our need for other humans in our life can go unmet.

Ideally, we have relationships that are based on mutual respect, tolerance, empathy, and appropriate boundaries. That doesn't mean that there will be no conflict. It doesn't mean that there won't be longstanding disagreements about how our mutual lives are being conducted. It doesn't mean that we must share our feelings all the time, and it doesn't mean that everybody has to understand where we're coming from and what we're going through.

Part of cultivating and understanding our relationships and the various dynamics of human interaction is understanding that individuals receive and process information differently.

My daughter and her husband both decided to take to take the same online IQ test. Fortunately, the result was about the same for both of them, but the most interesting outcome was my daughter's observation of her husband's different approach to some of the questions from the way that she worked through them. They are equal in the test's measure of intelligence, but not equal in the way they arrive at their intelligent answers.

We are sometimes tempted to write off the criticism we get from others as "Hey, it's just my personality". You know what? There is probably a lot of truth to that. That doesn't give you an excuse to be a jerk or have chronically bad relationships, but it might take some pressure off of some chronically tense relationships.

How do you sort out the source of relationship problems? Get a legitimate assessment of your personality. You'll find lots of free or fee personality tests online that might give you some insight into your personality. And that might point to some reasons why there is conflict in your relationships whether those be at the office, at home, or around the table at Thanksgiving.

If you really want to know more about your personality profile, consider paying for a personality test from a qualified mental health practitioner. As a police officer, I have been subjected to mandatory psychological testing and evaluation multiple times in my career. I can't say that knowing the results of these tests has been life-changing, but I can say I didn't find anything in the results that I disagreed with. Of course, my testimonial has nothing to do with whether any of those tests are scientifically valid, I'm just saying I can see their value and trust their accuracy.

Personality types have been categorized for centuries by various philosophers. The categories are generally broad most notoriously the astrological signs of the zodiac. Taking a few characteristics that seem to be true and assigning yourself to a category can lead to a self-fulfilling prophecy – "Oh, I'm a Libra, we're like that ya' know". I find that terribly unhealthy and that's why I recommend something that has some science to it rather than superstition.

What you're after is more than general labels like moody or thoughtful or artistic. You want to know how you look at the world in order to contrast to the way that other people do – especially those people with whom you must interact regularly.

A google search for "personality types" will give you several lists of categories. Books like *How We Love* and *Five Love Languages* will give some worksheets that can provide insights into how relationships can clash between personality types.

The more extensive the test (in other words the

more responses it asks for) the more reliable the results. In a sit down sessions with a psychologist, for example, he or she might show you a picture and ask you to tell what you think about it, show you ink blot patterns, an unfinished cartoon panel, use flash cards with various problems, ask you to remember a sequence of things, and do a multiple choice test (well, it's not a "test", but an "instrument") then evaluate your responses according to standardized and scientifically validated standards.

Some multiple-choice instruments will only indicate if you are "out of bounds" compared to most people who have taken the test. Some employers will test for specific factors like honesty or the likelihood of staying with the company.

Be careful that you don't waste time on the silly online ones that tell you which Disney character you are or which Sesame Street Muppet you're most like.

My hope, if you decide to do some research on personality types, is that you develop an awareness that people don't always think the way you think or see the world the way you do. What does that get you? It gets you an understanding that you might actually agree with a person who seems adversarial, but that you're approaching a situation from different perspectives.

Conflicts may not go away, but if you approach things with a greater expectation that you might need to communicate differently due to innate differences to get on a common wavelength, you can have better success at getting along with others.

Strategy # 3: Rehearsal

Facing the unknown is always adrenaline producing. For some, that's exciting and to be sought after, but for most of us, it can lead to shakes and stomach aches.

The reason truly new events are stressful is that the brain must take time to process all of the sensory inputs, apply them to all memories to find something that provides guidance on how to handle this experience, then calculate alternatives.

We get literally millions of sensory inputs from our five senses every minute. Each input can trigger a memory or emotion associated with it. The brain does a generally good job of filtering through all that information so that it doesn't drag us down with an information overload. And, remember, most of that processing happens at a level you have no awareness of.

But just because you're not consciously aware of what your brain is thinking about on its own doesn't mean that you have no reaction to it. That linking brain of yours, with all its memories and emotions, can be responding emotionally and behaviorally and make you feel things that you don't know understand why you're feeling.

The other thing that can happen is that the brain can disregard information that would actually be helpful in making a decision. This is referred to as inattentional blindness. A well-known video exercise is known as the invisible gorilla video. It features a squad of athletes passing a basketball around. The viewer is instructed to count the number of passes of the basketball as the team busily plays.

Most viewers concentrate closely on the movement of the ball and do not see a gorilla-suited individual entering the scene. When reviewing the video they often refuse to believe the gorilla was there at all during their first view!

Because of the popularity of the video, it has lost some of its value, for if the viewer knows to look for the gorilla then the gorilla will be seen. But all of us have experienced this type of blindness. If you've ever been in a crash or near-crash you know this experience. Where did that car/pedestrian/cyclist come from?

One of the reasons for the popularity of body-worn cameras for police officers is that witnesses and the officers themselves often don't recall some critical part of a scene. It isn't because they are poor observers or lying, but we have human limitations in how we process information – even things that are obvious to a person watching the same event unfold.

So, back to the point. We can reduce our blindness by learning what to focus on and attend to, especially in situations we expect to encounter and know have caused us distress in the past. We can reduce the stress of a situation by imagining ways we might act in a situation. Make it a positive outcome. Consider a variety of ways a challenge might be faced and resolved.

Why can this help? The brain tries to rely on past experiences when processing how the body should behave in reaction to a situation. If the situation has been faced before, the brain will default to the previous response and do it again. This is a positive thing in that it relieves a lot of strain from decision making by repeating what's already been learned. Imagine you had to take a new route home from work every day. That would cause you to have to do a lot more thinking than the robotic way you head home every day now with very little thought.

It is important to train the mind and body to respond quickly and effectively to emergencies. This is why we have fire drills. Practicing creates some "ruts" in our brain that decisions can fall into without reinventing a response. This makes our response faster and more accurate.

There are a couple of downsides to this brain function. One is that our brain might access the wrong template for reacting – such as grabbing a sharp falling object instead of letting it drop when are conditioned to grab anything falling. But the bottom line is that practice makes dealing with things easier. The more rehearsal you do, and the more variations you consider, the better you'll handle whatever comes your way. And, by the way, the practice can be just mental.

Learning – that is, rehearsal and practice – is most effective the more senses that are used in the process. When I was teaching college I strongly encouraged my students to take old-fashioned, handwritten notes. I also encouraged questions and discussion. In that way, they engaged with my lecture not just visually and audibly, but by touch and repetition as they processed information and wrote it down on the page. By engaging in discussion and asking questions, they made further memories and neural pathways that included social and emotional engagement.

But the brain, as we have seen, is so amazing that it can rehearse all by itself. Studies show that just imagining practicing a skill like shooting a basket, shooting at a target, or playing a keyboard can improve those skills to a significant percentage.

Although we can see that mental and physical rehearsal has the advantage of preparing our actions and reactions, there is danger in rumination.

Rumination is the rolling over and over of a thought or question in your head. Again, this can be healthy and productive, as you grasp for the hope of some sudden insight and solution, but it can also be a mechanism for making you crazy.

If you haven't come up with an answer to a question you've been thinking and thinking and thinking about, one suggestion is to create a temporary solution regardless of how ludicrous it is. If, for example, you are flummoxed over how to pay the bills and it is keeping you awake at night, decide that you can make enough money by getting a job as a Hollywood stunt man. Your brain will know that there is no need to keep pondering the problem now that it is solved, and you can make a note to revisit the matter later with more realistically.

As you engage in introspection about coping with our stress and anxiety, being aware of the triggers and stressors is a very important exercise. The value of recognizing circumstances that register high on your stress-o-meter is that you can work backward from the stress onset to identify precursors.

Precursors are the stairsteps to your anxiety event. Once you can recognize when you're climbing those stairs, you can use your logic brain to avoid the impulsive stress response and head off an unpleasant experience.

By identifying precursors, you can rehearse your response. For example, if a relative or co-worker always gets under your skin, rehearse your response to their presence or the behavior, words, or facial expressions that disrupt your emotional stability.

One of my triggers is getting advice that is either patently obvious and unnecessary, or assumes my ignorance. That's a character flaw of ego that I struggle with. I try to take a pause, avoid a smart retort, and say "thanks for pulling me up on that", a phrase I learned from a character building program used in the Missouri prison system for life sentenced inmates in honor housing. Accepting criticism and correction, even if misguided, is a much healthier way of coping than using a toothbrush sharpened into a knife to stab the other person. If it can work on inmates convicted of murder, it might work on you!

When practicing responses, they can be verbal or behavioral, but should always be in accordance with the biblical counsel of Proverbs 15:1 *A soft answer turneth away wrath: but grievous words stir up anger.* We think that "winning" with a strong, sassy comeback will make us feel better, but it is much better do something that will bring you peace of mind and move on from that moment.

Journal about it later to process your response and determine if you need to rehearse a different response.

Strategy # 4: Fellowship

No man is an island, says the poet. **We are wired and designed to connect and coexist with other humans.** Many would argue that we are better off with a dog for a companion. There is a lot of research that shows that pets can provide mental health benefits, but I am still going to advocate for human fellowship as most important.

For the first responder, finding friends who truly understand in what kind of world the police officers live is close to impossible. The good news is that we don't need a cast of friends, all of whom "get it" when it comes to the police perspective. For those reading who aren't in the emergency business, you have the same challenges. Nobody really appreciates what your day looks like, what kind of boss you have, or the stresses and strains of your work – even work you love (and even work you hate).

We need to find friends who are supportive, congenial, enjoyable to be around, challenging, with one or two confidantes in that group. You can find these in recreation leagues, support groups, faith groups, and coffee shops. But, we also need to examine the relationships that we have that are enemies of our peace of mind.

That doesn't mean that anybody we disagree with gets "unfriended", or that people who seem to rely on us or need our support should be walled out of our life. But it might. Really toxic personalities that create distress in our lives need to be managed. The book *Boundaries* by Henry Cloud can be very helpful in thinking through how much energy we should be giving away to people who hurt us.

One way to think about your relationships is to use a mind mapping technique. Write your name in a circle on a large piece of paper. You can use a notebook-sized paper and pen, but the bigger the paper and the bigger the marker, the bigger and more creative your thinking will be. Now write the names in a random pattern around the paper surrounding your name. Leave room for comments, because the next step is to write words that you associate with the person.

You don't need to worry about spelling, making sentences, or whether the word is a verb, noun, adjective, or adverb. Just be spontaneous. Use different colors, different sized letters. If the feeling is strong, make the word BIGGER. Then, draw lines between the names who have a link to each other aside from their link to you.

When you're done writing, sit back and look at the themes and how those themes connect to people in your life. Did you have an awareness of your emotional connection to each person? Does the interconnection of relationships complicate things? With in-laws and step-relatives things can get complicated, but don't make the mistake of thinking things have to remain the way they've always been. Re-arranging priorities among friends and family can be painful in the short term, but essential in the long term.

As a final note, don't forget your "friends" on social media. How much garbage and negativity does your **Facebook** bring into your life? That is totally within your control to manage. We don't manage it, by the way, by making a witty, sarcastic, insulting, or nice long rational post in response. Don't. Just don't. Step away, block, ignore, or otherwise reduce your exposure to the unpleasantness that often happens on Facebook.

Strategy # 5: Structured Introspection

A common characteristic of worriers is **spiraled thinking** and constant self-talk that never resolves. (Dr. Dave Stoop's *You Are What You Think* is a good book on self-talk).

Spiraling thinking is repetitive thoughts that go over the same territory over and over. You drive your partner nuts with the same subject. You bring it up when there's the slightest connection from somebody else's conversation. It keeps you up at night. You ruminate over things that happened long ago. Sometimes your father's or mother's voice in your head guides the internal conversation with accusations, put-downs, doubts, and strong opinions. It is a broken record, skipping to the same track without finishing a song.

One way to combat this disorganized and intrusive process is to become intentional about it. As Dr. Carlson writes in You *Can Be Happy No Matter What*, your thoughts are yours and you can learn to control them. We often think we are at the mercy of random thoughts and random emotions. We are if we have allowed ourselves to be conditioned that way.

However, we can practice controlling intrusive thoughts by choosing not to think about them, or by distracting our thinking process. Some distraction techniques include imagining our thoughts floating away, being locked in a vault to open later, or showing up on a chalkboard which we erase until the board is blank.

Things that we think about have some importance to our brains somewhere in our neural network, so we may not want to try to completely extinguish the topic. We take control by being intentional about when and how we'll think about these things. Making lists, drawing mind maps, talking through them with a friend or therapist at a scheduled time builds a structure that lets thoughts in or keeps them at bay.

Even things like sadness and grief can be corralled. Give yourself ten minutes to ponder or feel. Make it only every Thursday. You'll be surprised that you can **schedule and limit the time that you give to distressing thoughts**.

Doing things that keep you too busy for unproductive thinking such as exercise, visiting with loved ones, playing a board game or doing a puzzle can also give you a vacation from troubling thoughts.

Strategy # 6: Shifting Your Locus of Control

Stress is, in one sense, just your body's way of trying to regain control after the fear of losing it. Our attitudes and outlooks about who or what is controlling our lives or limiting our freedom can reduce stress by exerting control over how we process our environment.

There is a classic experiment in which a dog is placed in a cage from which there is no escape. After a period of time, the screen serving as the cage of the roof is unlocked. Now, all the dog has to do is push the low screen and he is free! Because the dog has learned from prior experience that there is no use trying, he doesn't and remains caged even though freedom is just a nose away.

This gave rise to the concept of **learned helplessness**, which is a state of believing there is no escape or solution to a problem even though the answer might be very realistic. I am reminded of the account in the Bible of Jesus' healing of the disabled man at the pool of Bethesda. Among many waiting to get into the mystical healing waters was a man who had been disabled, and therefore presumably a despised, beggar, who was waiting for the waters to ripple indicating that an angel had visited and, as the story was told to him, the first person in the waters would be healed. For a mobility impaired man, this presented an obvious problem.

Jesus walked over to him and asked: "Do you want to be healed"? The man launched into an explanation of his problems and how he can't get into the pool. But he didn't answer Jesus' question: Do you want to be healed? Have you given up hope of any control over your life? Are you comfortable in your misery and afraid of trying again? Is your story of misery more compelling than a story of trying one more thing?

Our ideas about what constrains our life is referred to as our **locus of control**. Studies have shown that individuals with an internal locus of control have greater measures of happiness and success. Those with an external locus of control live with a self-fulfilling prophecy that things are beyond their control and the best they can do is float along with whatever current comes along.

An intentional awareness of what our hopes and dreams are, and what stands between that and our future reality, is the first step in shifting our locus of control to internal rather than external. One way of moving in that direction is simply making a list or journaling about what we really want. This should be weighted to how we want to feel and be in relationships but can include a change in employment, health, or some life adventure. Then, using three columns, write down what is in the way of your goals on one outer column, what is in your favor in the other outer column, and what one or two things would get you closer to your goal in the middle column. Now you have a record of facts, not merely feelings, that you can use as a tool to bring about changes in your circumstances, your perceived limitations, or your attitudes about your situation.

The most important thing in thinking about changes in life is to be deliberate in including things that make you feel uncomfortable. Discomfort just means you're getting out of comfort, and very little change arises out of comfort!

Strategy # 7: Neutralize the Lizard Brain

We briefly visited the idea that distress arises from our lizard brain's perception of threat which then robs the body's resourced to marshal for the F3 response. That lizard brain is great, we love him, because he just wants us to live and who can blame him! Like any little ball of energy and single-mindedness, the lizard brain can be trained a little bit too. We don't have to allow fear to be our primary emotion, coloring every life experience. I'm going to make a few suggestions for opening the window of joy a little wider.

The lizard brain cares nothing about happiness, he wants alertness instead. He doesn't urge us to stop and smell the rose, he says to watch out for bees. He doesn't care to have us gaze at the blue sky, he wants us to look closely at that stick on the sidewalk to be sure it isn't a snake. You see, negative interpretations of incoming sensory messages have immediate survival value. Positive messages have long-term well-being value. But, remember, **the lizard brain only wants us to live for the next minute** – anything after that is none of his concern.

There are plenty of brain functions that process pleasure, warmth, nice memories, sensuality, and other things of beauty and sweetness. But they, like other body functions, are subject to hijack by the lizard brain. We can get around that!

Imagine that the lizard brain is tucked deep in the base of our brain, closer to the back of the neck than the front of the head. Now the linking brain can be imagined as the bulk of our noodle in the middle of everything, with the logic brain being lodged up against our forehead. That's sort of accurate, but, most importantly, it helps us visualize how we can regain control of our F3. When time allows (in a panic, the lizard brain takes over – there's no time to process and think, just act in the power of adrenaline!) literally place your fingers on the base of the back of your head, then draw a curved arrow along the center of your head, tracing along the top, passing the linking brain, and coming to rest pointing at your forehead – the logic brain.

Bring your thoughts along with your fingers! When you feel fear, panic, distress, anger, shock, distrust, or anything "negative", bring those feelings to your logic brain to analyze them. What is causing this feeling? We might start by thinking about our senses. Is there a smell, a touch, a movement, a place, a sound, a temperature, a circumstance that your lizard brain associates with danger or threat? (By the way, the lizard brain doesn't care if it's a threat to your body or a threat to your ego and self-esteem – the response is the same!)

You might identify the alley you just walked by as similar to the alley where you once got assaulted years ago. The smell of a distant fire might trigger a deep-seated reaction from a fiery crash you were involved in. A whiff of perfume or cologne might remind you of the person who broke your heart. These cues can be at a very subtle level beyond our sense of awareness, but the lizard never forgets. Just remember to point your finger at the feeling (that lizard brain location), then drag those feelings through your linking brain to the logic brain and analyze them there.

You don't have to answer the riddle at that moment. What you can do is to tell the lizard brain "thanks for watching out for me, but I'm fine. I'm safe. That's just a stick, not a snake. There's no one in the alley. I have a flashlight and a cell phone so the darkness can't harm me", and so on. **Make your logic brain take over and calm the lizard brain**. Making a positive, fact-based conclusion about a threat feeling will neutralize the negative.

Strategy # 8: Increasing Positivity

As we mentioned in strategy # 7, there is no immediate survival value in positive and happy thoughts. Some of us are more naturally happy and optimistic than others. Some of us used to be and got the stuffing knocked out of us. Some, like your author, spent a lot of years dealing with negative, violent, dishonest people and began to believe that was normal. For people like that (myself included) a discipline of creating positives is essential.

The amazing thing about that lizard brain that seems to cause so much trouble is that he is buried in a dark place and completely dependent on information coming in. The same is true of the linking brain as well. Have you ever cried from a sad movie? Didn't you know it was just a story with mere actors? You did, but your brain didn't. Sad = cry. Scary movies? Same thing.

 A good friend of mine opened a private counseling practice after finishing his doctorate in psychology. He tells of one of his first clients – a financially stable woman who lived in a quiet mountain setting but reported being inexplicably sad. Asking her about her daily routine she responded that she liked listening to the police scanner, watching soap operas, and listening to country music. The quick diagnosis? **Vicarious depression**.

Her lizard brain couldn't tell that the fight and crash calls causing tense voices and sirens on the scanner weren't about his owner. Or the break up between SueEllen and Royce on the Sands of Our Young Lives daytime soap wasn't the severing of an ego defining personal relationship, or that the momma who prayed but her young'n went to prison wasn't about a loved one.

The simple formula for countering the negatives in life? **Increase the positive**. And yes, that can include saying corny affirmations to yourself in the mirror. It includes sticky note reminders on the fridge, flowers on the table, jokes from the internet, and giving compliments to see smiles appear.

Even fake smiles create positive feelings. A famous study showed that clenching a pencil between your teeth mimics the smile muscles in the face and causes more positive feelings. There may be some truth to the idea of "fake it 'til you make it"!

A second, powerful positivity is **gratitude therapy**. I spoke recently with a man who had come from visiting his damaged home in the Houston area ravaged by Hurricane Harvey. He talked about how his home's damage could have been worse, how the neighbors and disaster relief volunteers were working hard, and how he was happy he was alive to see it all. Talk about a positive attitude! The old hymn says:

Count your many blessings name them one by one, and

I know that's easy advice to give and we sometimes don't want to hear it – but why? Because we want to wallow in our misery a little longer. We want to retain the right to complain and blame. We find it easier to look at people who we think have it better than we do at the moment, rather than realize there are a lot of people who would be jealous of us and our situation.

Gratitude is a discipline. By definition, we must engage in thankfulness when we feel least thankful.

Thirdly, under the category of infusing more positives into your life, is music. Choose music by its beauty and its words, or its association with good memories. You might like a hard beat, raw lyrics, and tunes that speak to your hard life, but for positive therapy, these are not constructive choices. You need less expression of your feelings and more infusion of hope.

I recall a colleague who lost his wife to a long and

difficult illness. Our offices shared a wall and month after month I heard funeral music playing and I knew his wife's image was bouncing around on his screen saver. We can understand being immersed in grief for a long time, and I don't advocate artificially shortening the process. My colleague never gave himself permission to have guilt-free joy along the way, and a few years later he was dead by his own hand.

Music has a power that has long been recognized as transformative. Might as well transform in a positive way.

Strategy # 9: Exercise for the Brain

We will talk about pharmaceuticals later, but it is now common knowledge that the effectiveness of **physical activity can equal or surpass some medications for anxiety and depression**. Remember that bath of stress chemistry that the lizard brain uncorks during F3? That stuff gets toxic after it serves its purpose. The body flushes that those harsh chemicals out and resumes "normal" by using up the adrenaline chemistry during the F3 if there is a fight or a flight. The large muscle groups burn it up for power.

What if we have the F3 response but no actual fight or flight? Then the chemistry has to slowly metabolize and get diluted and processed out. This takes recovery time, with the help of some body chemistry that also helps as an "antidote" to the harmful effects of the flooded system.

The classic modern stress problem isn't with occasional high levels of stress during emergencies, but the constant lower stress that creates a relentless drip of the chemistry into our system. Without physical activity to burn up the adrenaline cocktail, or a significant time of stress-free rest and restoration, the chemistry continues to create stress responses that rob the normal body systems of their necessary elements. But what about that antidote chemistry? The problem here is that the adrenaline chemistry is virtually unlimited, while the metabolizing chemistry can be used up when constantly drawn upon.

A solution? Fake fight and flight, i.e. jogging, aerobics, dance, walking, SOMETHING! Don't think this means going into triathlon training. Find one of the thousands of exercise websites and choose something that works for you. Yoga and tai chi are great, a stationary bicycle is great. Invest time and money in this process. It is worth it.

Now a quick word about weight. Fat is fatal and depressing. I remember when my family physician said that I wasn't technically obese. What a relief! I appreciate his diplomacy, but a better smack in the face might have been to tell me I needed to lose fifty pounds. After my diabetes diagnosis, I later lost 65 pounds.

My secret? Math. I found what my resting calorie use was, added what calories I could burn from safe exercise (something that wouldn't blow out my knees!) and started counting calories. It takes roughly a 3000 calorie deficit between what you burn up and take in to lose 1 pound. Most of us can easily reduce calories by 300 daily. That soda or mocha frapp, for example. Keep doing that until the math is right and you lose weight.

And, of course, we can't talk about exercise and weight control without talking about nutrition. I am convinced that a balanced diet with protein, fruits and vegetables, reduced sugar and carbohydrate intake along with plenty of water during the day.

Brain fog or **brain fatigue** – memory problems and lack of focus – can be the result of many factors, but one aspect is possibly nutrition imbalance. Avoid trendy fad diets and consult a nutrition expert as part of your coping strategy for anxiety, stress, or depression.

Before we leave this section about how we treat our body, let me emphasize two very fundamental exercises that I recommend being done frequently, even multiple times during the day: **breathing** and **stretching**.

Regulating your breathing (and thus your blood pressure and pulse) is an important discipline because the lizard brain will hijack even this basic body process if allowed. Athletes, soldiers, and emergency workers recognize the value of this tactic. In my circle, it is referred to as combat breathing. More extensive relaxation breathing, when you have quiet time, is described at this Veteran Affairs site:

https://www.va.gov/vetsinworkplace/docs/em_eap_exe rcise_breathing.asp. In fact the VA has a lot of good information on PTSD.

For a quick focus, follow these steps:

Take a deep breath, preferably through the nose (from the diaphragm, like your choir teacher taught you!) If your shoulders go way up, your breathing is too shallow and you're filling less of your lungs). Breathe in for a count of 1, 2, 3, 4.

Hold that as you count 4, 3, 2, 1

Breathe out through the mouth with a pushhhhhhh for a count of 1, 2, 3, 4 (with an optional conditioning word like peace or breeze, etc.)

And repeat for a total of four times. So it's 4 in, hold 4, out 4 for 4 cycles. If you want to take your pulse before and after, you will likely find that your heart rate has slowed.

While we are on the subject of breathing, let's talk about **panic attacks**. These episodes are frightening and sudden, giving a feeling of doom and loss of control. As soon as you feel an anxiety attack – you can learn when to expect them or what the **precursors** to an attack are – it is important to learn to talk yourself through it.

The sense that one is dying from a heart attack is a common sensation among panic attack sufferers. When in doubt, you should get to the emergency room and have a physician sort it out. In either case, remaining in control of yourself is the key so that you can make a decision to carry on.

One recommendation is to remember to trace that line from your lizard brain to the logic brain and try to think more clearly. Getting back a feeling of being grounded, rather than feeling out of control, is helpful.

Tell yourself that you're still in control and safe and that you'll be back to normal soon. Intentionally feel your feet against the earth – feeling literally grounded, and begin to focus on all of your senses. Pick out three things you can see, then three things you can hear, three you can touch, and three you can smell or taste. If you get stuck looking for three things, move to the next. Use combat breathing to re-regulate your system, then find a safe place to rest or get assistance in getting medical care.

In terms of exercise, if you aren't up for jumping jacks and jogging, simple stretches can help get out some kinks, get some blood to your muscle groups, and increase your sense of vigor. There are books and articles on stretching, but I will offer a very simple formula. By the way, there are some recent articles I've read saying that stretching as a warm-up for exercise has little benefit for athletic performance or injury prevention. I don't care. Moving what you have is always good!

Here's my routine. I like to start with a standing stretch, feet on the floor in a solid stance then simply reach as high as I can, slowly and very aware of how my body is feeling. I sway left and right in an arc with my hands up, then bend over to touch the floor with my fingertips. I then cross my legs at the ankle and repeat my arm and upper body movement, taking care not to fall now that my feet are tangled and positioned with less stability. I then get my solid stance back and, with hands to sides or positioned on my hips I close my eyes and do a slow head and neck roll, once clockwise and once the opposite. After that, it's kind of free-lance movement as I think of what needs to be moved and unkinked.

Another technique I enjoy and use is also simple and can be done almost anywhere. It is a progressive tension and relaxation regimen that has the benefit of teaching our body how tension versus relaxation feels. Standing is preferred but you can do it while driving or sitting at your desk. Clench your toes, the tighten your muscles in your feet, then ankles, then lower legs, thighs, buttocks, chest, arms, fingers, neck, and head. Now crank everything up one more notch!

Now, starting head first, release each set of muscles to relaxation. Neck, shoulders, arms and hands, chest, stomach, buttocks, thighs, legs, feet and imagine that tension melting through your feet into the floor and breathe out slowly.

If you practice being aware of what tensed muscles feel like, you can do a quick check throughout the day and you may find, as I do, that you're all knotted up for no apparent reason. Now you can take a minute or two and lighten your load a bit. It will be refreshing and help prevent that worn out fatigue feeling you have at the end of the day even though you don't remember working hard enough to be sore and tired. Your muscles, tense for F3, are working! Give them a break!

Strategy # 10: Have a Talk With Your Enemy

Although I didn't get my counseling advice from Simon and Garfunkel, I think of the words "hello darkness, my old friend, I've come to talk to you again", it is the germ of a good idea.

We often believe we are passive recipients of feelings and seem surprised by visiting emotions, especially intense ones that cause distress, anger, and fear. One strategy to deal with these invasive feelings is to give them a name and call them out. "Hey Fear, what do you want? Are you trying to help me? Teach me something? Well, I don't have time for you right now. Come back later".

Creating a dialog with your feelings, separating them from yourself for a moment and exercising dominion over them, can reduce anxiety by increasing our sense of control. Our sense of lack of control is at the core of distress.

Strategy # 11: A Unified Life Philosophy

Research indicates that one of the greatest assets a person can have to be resilient when facing adversity is having a belief system through which to view the world. As a Christian, I can offer the fundamentals of my biblical understanding that provide a framework for coping: God cares about you and knows you; there is more to life than the present moment; God's will and purpose is often hidden but always real.

For me, this gives a sense of manageability to my life even in the worst of circumstances. Understanding the temporary condition of my existence puts experiences and suffering in some perspective. And knowing that I don't have to understand everything or figure everything out allows me to know that the answers to the great questions of life are discoverable, whether in this life or the next.

My understanding of God's work in the world includes his grace to allow people to ignore him and believe what they will. This is known in theology as **common grace**, the blessings that all humans can enjoy regardless of whether they acknowledge God or not. Humans can have a measure of joy and happiness while believing in other religions or even none. Despite what we often want to think as Christians that only we can have contentment, others can find a satisfying life (at least in this present world) with differing beliefs.

The importance (again, in the temporal world) is having some sense of unity and direction about life's purpose and meaning. This, too, is related to our sense of control.

For the Christian, it is that God is in control and therefore I can trust in that. For the Buddhist, perhaps the idea that we can separate ourselves from the desires of the world and therefore have nothing to lose provides comfort in times of distress. For the non-deist, perhaps the thought that you can only do so much and the rest is just luck might be the simple resolution to complicated questions.

Feeling like the universe is picking on us can lead to self-doubt and depression. A person whose home is destroyed in a tornado that destroys dozens of homes will feel less unfairness than the person who is in a crash with a drunk driver. The lament of "why me" is stronger when it seems fate has singled you out. It's easier to take when there are other victims. This may be why we get some comfort in the normalizing knowledge that we are not alone in whatever bad circumstance comes our way.

For those who want a booster of encouragement about God's care, a quick internet search for Bible verses on peace, joy, comfort, grief, or other burden can give assurance that you're not facing anything that hasn't been suffered and overcome before.

Strategy # 12: Take a sabbath

In our western culture, we value activity and we like to boast about how many hours we work and how few hours we sleep. More and more research into sleep deprivation is shedding light on how failure to rest well is dangerous in a variety of ways.

The biblical pattern in the account of creation is a day of rest every week. We see Jesus frequently headed for the mountains and leaving the crowds behind. This pattern of rest can be extended to our intentional management of stress and anxiety.

In addition to sleep, we can engage in restorative and restful activities that are helpful in reducing stress and anxiety. Here are some ideas:

- **Prayer and Meditation** – For the Christian, the model for praying is best found in the little acronym ACTS. A is for adoration. When we start out with our demands and complaints, we can lose focus of our primary license to pray in the first place, which is God's kindness, grace, an invitation to pray. C is for confession. Acknowledging our failings, engaging in forgiveness, and taking inventory of our lives, motives, and actions is a powerful connection to our most honest selves – the self our God already knows all about. T is for thanksgiving, which is the opportunity to engage in that gratitude therapy I mentioned earlier. This is great for perspective building. It reminds us that we've gotten through hard times before, and of all the opportunities we have for victory and joy in times to come. Finally, the S is for supplication, a fancy word for asking. We ask first on behalf of the needs of others. Again, this is a time of perspective as we join in the knowledge that others are in need. Finally, we ask for the desires of our own heart and mind, in the faith, persistence, and wisdom that the Bible teaches should be our prayerful attitude.

Meditation has been celebrated for its ability to change our brain. The secular, new age or eastern religion foundation for meditation is to empty oneself. For the Christian, meditation is to fill oneself with God's truth through scripture and prayer.

The practice of **mindfulness** is being aware of being, of contemplating only the   moment, or contemplating a specific sensation such as what one is holding in one's hand. It makes no judgment. You can find mindfulness methods easily with an internet search.

Speaking as a Christian, I urge caution in considering this method because its essence contradicts essential biblical teachings of the centricity of God over man, eternity over the temporary, and the prohibition of making anything sacred that is idolatrous.

- **Hobbies**. Some hobbies seem mindless, but that really is the point when it comes to relief from stress. Others direct effort (and stress!) in healthy ways. Others promote fellowship and teamwork. Others have a service aspect where we give to others in a way that warms our own heart. All focus our attention on new things or routine things that provide stimulation or comfort. Unless they interfere with our relationships or finances, hobbies are an important way to relax or diffuse our stress.
- **Vacations.** Getting away from work or any environment with lots of triggers for stress and trauma is important for life balance.

Unfortunately, vacations can be stressors when the agendas are rushed, conflict with the wishes of our fellow travelers, cost too much, or are too short. I love small trips, but it can take two to three weeks away from a stressful workplace to reach a relaxed state of mind and body chemistry

I want to include fasting in the vacation category. This may go more with meditation, since withdrawing from anything you regularly do will cause discomfort, one should use that discomfort – such as hunger – to call one into a state of prayer or awareness.
You can fast from coffee, television, Facebook (highly recommended!) or any other pleasure or distraction in order to focus on positive growth.

Strategy # 13: Touch

Human contact is essential to normal life. Hugs, handshakes, arms around a shoulder, pats on the back all create a brain chemistry boost of positive feelings (unless the touch triggers unpleasant memories or thoughts, of course).

If you aren't around affectionate people, pets have proven to be of great benefit to mental health.

Self-touching can be therapeutic as well. Massaging your own head, tugging your hair, or pressing hairbrush bristles to your scalp can stimulate circulation. Warm baths, oil, and steam rooms are a sensual experience that also stimulates the skin.

Professional massage, reflexology, or even a makeover can provide some human contact and professional attention to the body that relaxes the body and, therefore, affects brain chemistry and stress in a positive way.

Strategy # 14: Professional Therapy

Getting professional help to improve your life makes a lot of sense. For a variety of reasons, going to a counselor is a difficult decision. Let's talk about why that is so.

First of all is the stigma attached to being a person with a problem can't solve or can't handle. We all want to be in control, competent, wise, and independent. Somehow going to a counselor is different than going to a doctor in the minds of most folks. But this shouldn't stop you from considering professional therapy if there is a possibility that your life could be significantly improved.

Secondly, finding a counselor can be a daunting task. Let's talk about the different kinds of counselors available to you.

The most highly trained brain health expert is the

psychiatrist. A psychiatrist is a medical doctor who has attained a specialty in psychiatry through additional schooling and experience. Because it is not the most lucrative of medical specialties, access to psychiatric care can be difficult and their caseloads are typically high. The two major advantages of psychiatric care are that they are able to diagnose and discover organic brain illness, and they are able to prescribe medications to remedy physical deficiencies of brain disorders.

There are many behavior abnormalities that are a result of chemical imbalance, brain damage including traumatic brain injury (TBI), and diseases that destroy brain function. Without medical diagnostics, these behaviors are sometimes wrongly treated as an emotional problem or personality defect.

I can tell you two stories to illustrate. The first is about me as a young police officer arriving at the scene of a vehicle crash. A woman and her young son were in one badly damaged car. As I arrived, the medics were getting the mother on a stretcher as she moaned in pain. The boy was still in the back seat and looked stunned. I assumed he was in a state of emotional numbness because of the overwhelming circumstances. Later I discovered that he sustained a fractured pelvis and his state of shock was due primarily to his physical injury.

The second was a friend of mine who was on staff as a pastor at the church I attended. One of the members was going through a destabilizing time of life and behaving badly. The pastor was called by the member's wife to help calm her husband. As the pastor arrived, the man's speech was disorganized and repetitive, and he was quite agitated. Unknown to the pastor, the man was having a stroke type episode that, thankfully, was recognized by a neighbor witnessing the encounter and an ambulance was called.

Medical doctors with other specialties are, of course, legally empowered to prescribe drugs for anxiety, depression, and other conditions where brain chemistry is a likely factor. Most of the drugs prescribed for mental health conditions are from non-psychiatrist physicians. With all due respect, a complete diagnosis and therapeutic plan don't happen and comprehensive treatment and non-drug approaches can be overlooked as a resolution to the patient's complaint.

After teaching a college class session in a section on juvenile delinquency and behavior treatment with pharmaceuticals, a student approached me after class in the empty classroom. She shared with me that she had been on anti-depressants since the age of twelve. She was now a college freshman. I asked what other therapy she had gotten, and how the dosage and effectiveness had been monitored during that time. She said she had been offered no counseling and she was taking the same dose and the same drug for the past six years! She went through her entire critical adolescent development without further attention to her reported depression!

The second most highly trained mental health

professional is the psychologist. This person has a doctorate in psychology and has undergone additional training, experience, and supervision before being licensed to practice. Psychologists also have a lot of knowledge of the anatomy and biology of mental disorders but, in most states, are not authorized to prescribe medication. They will, however, be very knowledgeable about prescription drugs used to treat some symptoms and causes of mental illness and can make well-informed recommendations to your physician.

The next level of licensed mental health practitioner is the licensed counselor. This person has a graduate degree and many hours of supervision before being licensed. There are specialties such as marriage and family therapy, behavioral therapy, and many others. A licensed therapist or counselor may also choose areas of specialty based on their interests and experience.

The term "licensed" is an official status granted by your state and the oversight agencies for each type of practice to assure the consumer that the licensed person has an acceptable level of competence. This typically also requires the licensed person to obtain continuing education to maintain their legal status.

Another area of graduate-level licensure is the licensed social worker whose practice includes case management and institutional work, but who may engage in individual counseling as well.

For those with less than a graduate (master's) degree, there are specialties in which a person can get accreditation such as substance abuse or specific types of therapy methods.

At least in my state (Colorado), and presumably this is fairly standard in the U.S., the word "licensed" is the key to some level of assurance of a person's basic education and competence. The words "counselor" and "therapist" have no official meaning in terms of the regulation of the person's practice. An unlicensed counselor or therapist may be a good choice, with the only problem being that insurance typically covers only licensed practitioners.

My regulatory oversight designates me as a "registered psychotherapist". In my case, this means that I have applied with my portfolio of experience and training to achieve the designation in order that my qualifications and any complaints or disciplinary action can be accessed through the state's regulatory agency. As a chaplain, my pastoral counseling is unregulated (to avoid church/state conflicts).

Many people turn first to their pastor for counseling. Unless a minister has obtained special training during their academic preparation, they may have little or no training or experience in dealing with mental health issues. A pastor who recognizes the limitations of their knowledge in the field of mental health will be ready to make a referral to a therapist for problems beyond their scope of knowledge (as would any therapist, by the way) and confine their counsel to encouragement, support, and educating their client in biblical truth as it applies to the problem the client presents.

Simplistic advice like "try harder, repent of your sin, read the Bible more, pray more" is indeed a formula that is sound and important and should be a part of any believer's efforts in problem-solving. Issues of depression – especially suicidal thoughts and attempts, domestic violence, substance abuse, and other complex behavior disorders need as much attention as diabetes or a broken rib.

When choosing a counselor, there is more than what kind of certificates and plaques are on the wall and how nice their office furniture is. For example, for those with concerns about PTSD, I highly recommend a therapist with expertise in trauma. Therapies that are based on the client talking through their experiences, so-called **"talk therapy"**, can, in my opinion, be harmful in treatment of PTSD. A PTSD sufferer doesn't need to merely re-visit their trauma without a plan to resolve their feelings and physical reactions to it.

Talk therapy can be helpful when a client has not

effectively explored or articulated their feelings and experiences, and with the guidance of a therapist, they can discover insights that can lead to new strategies for managing their feelings and relationships. For specific issues, it is fair to ask the therapist what the course of action will be and how long the process might be expected to take.

It is also fair to ask the therapist if their practice is in any conflict with your religious faith. If the therapist believes that all religion is "magical thinking", or if they are going to ask you to connect with your spirit guide or spirit animal, or engage in a meditative practice that is based on principles in opposition to your faith (and, of course, I'm talking primarily to my Christian readers, but others as well). A therapist should meet the client with respect to the client's cultural orientation, and explore conflicts if that is relevant to the therapeutic approach.

The therapeutic relationship is different than a physician's patient relationship. The interaction is more personal and mutual respect and trust are essential. That doesn't mean that we should always feel comfortable during therapy! The counselor is not there to be a friend or to avoid hurting your feelings or challenging your thinking. So, being offended by an exploration of a hard truth is a likely experience.

Your first visit to a counselor will be a review of your "presenting problem" – the reason you're there. Counselors regulated by their states are likely to be required to present you with a disclosure form that outlines some expectations. Confidentially is an essential ethic in counseling. Payment information and billing practices, including consequences of missed appointments, need to be clear. Many practices use audio or video recording of sessions. While this may seem invasive, it is an important safeguard for the therapist and the client, and may even be required by their insurer.

Your counselor will be a **mandatory reporter** for child abuse, so if you make a statement that indicates that you have put a child at risk, or if within a certain time frame you were victimized as a child, the counselor must report that or face criminal and civil penalties. Some states may make domestic violence a mandatory report, as well as elder abuse or for other protected persons.

Your counselor is also exempted from confidentiality if your life or the life of another is potentially at risk based on the information obtained during a session.

Strategy # 15: Pharmaceuticals

I was working in a pharmacy in high school when this new pain management drug came out. It was called ibuprofen, and could only be obtained by prescription. Now it is the most popular over the counter pain medicine. The point is, science marches on and brings us new techniques, appliances, and chemistry frequently.

Although my hope for anyone would be that they aren't dependent on a drug for the rest of their lives, and can avoid medicine whenever possible, the access we have to drugs that can save and improve our lives is a great blessing of modern life. I hope to be free from my diabetes medication and am making healthy choices in order to try, but it may be part of my life for a long time. So, my position is that a conservative approach to prescription medication is prudent, but avoiding a solution that a prescription can provide is foolish.

Since I emphasize that the stress and anxiety I've been addressing is a matter of body chemistry, it should be clear that when we aren't able to control that chemistry by means of thought and behavior control, we can explore in good conscience a remedy through medicine.

In an attempt to simplify an explanation of our brain's processes, let me use the illustration of making an electrical connection by touching two exposed wires to each other and causing a spark. That spark would depend on a number of factors such as the strength of electrical pulse in those wires, the content of the atmosphere at the time of contact, the thickness of the wires and insulation, and the duration of the contact. If there are flammable materials nearby, the spark can spread flame or cause smoke. For engineers trying to control the spark, its intensity, and duration for use in a motor, the experiments to perfect that connection would include changing various conditions.

Similarly, scientists have learned about the variables in the neural connections in the brain that are associated with transferring chemical messages about danger, stress, emotions, muscle and nerve responses, etc. Medicines to slow down or speed up connections have been developed to modify connections that are out of tune or to add or minimize some brain chemistry.

One of the challenges to medicine for brain health is the time it might take to discover if you've taken the right medicine in the right dose. It can take months to determine if a medicine is having the desired effect without intolerable side effects. Withdrawing from some medications can take time as well, then the process might have to start again. With some conditions, it can take as much as two years to find the right combinations and dosages.

Many folks **self-medicate** and that is always dangerous. The allure of borrowing somebody else's prescriptions, using alcohol or marijuana, or relying on herbal products causes many to experiment while their conditions worsen and they delay professional help. It helps us hide our problems and gives us a sense that maybe we are in control after all. The essential problem with self-medication with alcohol and other drugs is that the pain may be numbed or masked, but the problems persist and worsen.

A counselor who determines that a client has a substance dependency must deal with that first before they are fully able to explore the root problems.

A Few Concluding Remarks

I hope that these suggestions can help improve your life. They might nudge you toward a little better management of your brain and emotions, or they might provide a huge light of revelation that you can take control of your life! You might have discovered that you need to seek professional help and find encouragement to do that.

If you have a story about how this little book has changed your thinking or some suggestions about how I can improve the content or presentation, I'd love to hear from you. If you have some comments of criticism that aren't constructive and helpful, please keep them to yourself. I don't need negativity in my life!

Now to him who is able to do immeasurably more than all we ask or imagine, according to his power that is at work within us, to him be glory in the church and in Christ Jesus throughout all generations, for ever and ever! Amen.

Ephesians 3:20-21

ABOUT THE AUTHOR

Dr. Shults is a registered psychotherapist and pastoral counselor in Colorado. He served in law enforcement as a police executive until his retirement, and spent many years as a college professor and police academy trainer. He became a first responder chaplain in 2001 and has worked with injured police officers through a national organization. He and his music teacher wife have been married 38 years and have two amazing adult children and one exceptional granddaughter. He is the author of a number of books, including The Badge and The Brain, which is the topic of one of the training areas he offers through Shults Professional Services, LLC. Found on the web at www.joelshults.com.

www.ingramcontent.com/pod-product-compliance
Lightning Source LLC
Chambersburg PA
CBHW050832260726
48660CB00006B/2202